Finger Funatics

FINE MOTOR DEVELOPMENT PROGRAM

A Guide for Teachers Pre-School through First Grade

By Shannon Samulski

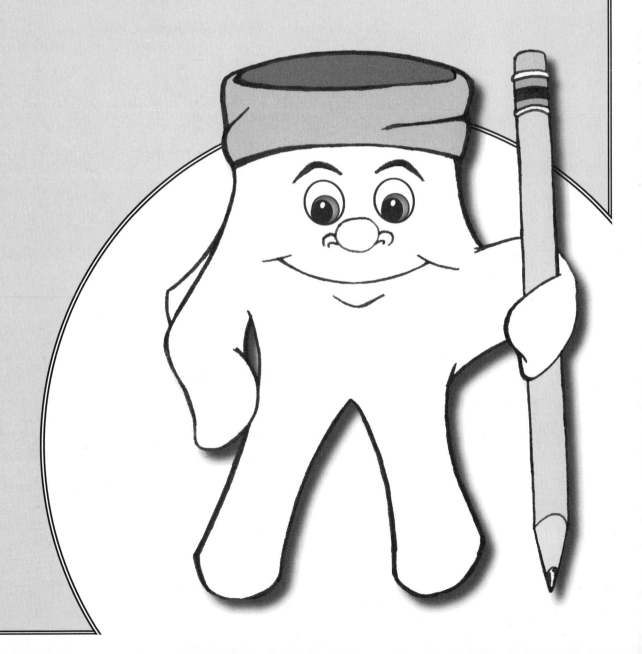

Publication Partnership

Wayne RESA
33500 Van Born Road
Wayne, MI 48184
(734) 334.1300
www.resa.net

Samulski Consulting, LLC
7051 Epping Drive
Canton, MI 48187
(734) 414.0425
www.fingerfunatics.com

First publication by Wayne RESA November, 2010

ISBN: 978–1–4507–3938–2

Printed in the United States of America
Wayne, Michigan

This book is printed on acid free paper

Editor ....Linda Wacyk
Graphic Designer ....Kate de Fuccio
Illustrator.............................Joshua Carpenter
Photographer....................John Kemski

Michigan Department of Education Great Parents, Great Start funding was used to support a portion of this work.

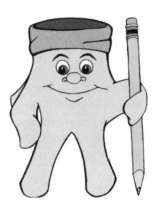

Dedication

This book is dedicated to my husband and our children.

Emma and Connor, you are my sun that shines every day and the

love I have for you both is indescribable. Brian, my soul mate and best friend,

thank you for all your support and for always believing in me.

Note: Some activities in the Finger Funatics program involve the use of small items and/or age-sensitive supplies found in most classrooms. The publisher and author assume no liability for the suggested exercises included in the Finger Funatics Program. Local school districts, teachers, and parents should exercise caution when recommending activities and should choose activities and materials appropriately based on age, aptitude and traits of the child(ren).

Table of Contents

Introduction

Welcome to the Finger Funatics Program!

Each year more and more students are coming to school with poorly developed fine motor skills. Often these same students have difficulty sitting still, coordinating eye and hand movement, holding a crayon or marker, cutting with scissors, or playing with puzzles. Their hands are weak and underdeveloped. They tend to avoid fine motor tasks. They may experience frustration when they write their names, zip their coats, open their milk cartons, putting on their boots or opening their backpacks.

Finger Funatics is an early intervention program that helps children to strengthen their hands and improve their fine motor skills. Through playful games, using age-appropriate materials, children spend just minutes a day building skills that help them succeed in school. Designed for use in preschool through first grade classrooms, *Finger Funatics* provides 50 kid-tested activities for school as well as home.

Pre- and Post-Assessment:

An easy to use pre-test helps the teacher determine which area of fine motor skills need intervention. A post-test is also included to help monitor progress and determine when a child has mastered a skill.

Finger Funatics can also be used with proficient students because activities include more challenging levels.

Classroom/Home Activities:

50 fun-filled, easy-to-teach activities are included using most materials that are readily available in the home or classroom. Each exercise or game has an "activity card" with the area of fine motor skills addressed, materials needed, and step-by-step directions.

In the classroom, activities can be completed in a variety of ways. After carefully modeling for the whole class, children can move through centers or work stations where they complete an activity independently. The teacher can stay at one station that requires more guided instruction or she can work individually with more needy children. Children requiring additional practice can take the activity card and materials home in a take home kit. Parents can work with their child to complete the activity.

The Finger Funatics Program helps students achieve the necessary fine motor skills for academic success.

Pre- and Post-Assessment

Directions for Pre-School and First Grade Fine Motor Student Pre- and Post-Evaluation

Developed by Shannon Samulski

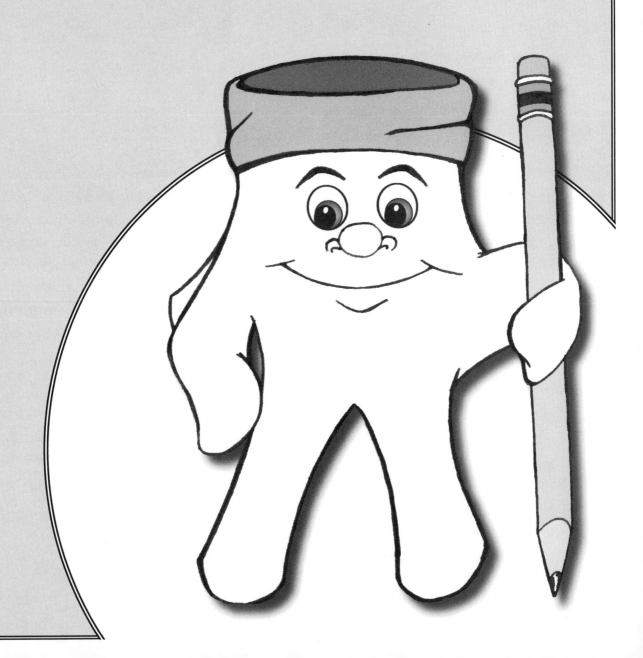

Finger Funatics Pre- and Post-Assessment

Materials needed to complete the assessments:

- [ ] 10 dried black beans
- [ ] timer
- [ ] container with 1-inch opening (e.g., empty medicine or water bottle)
- [ ] scissors
- [ ] blackline master circle on page 81
- [ ] pencil
- [ ] paper
- [ ] 10 1-inch blocks
- [ ] squeeze ball (pre-school)
- [ ] single hole punch (Kindergarten/Grade 1)
- [ ] individual student scoring card on page 16

The assessment can be used for an individual student or an entire class to determine the level of fine motor development. The follow areas are assessed:

- **Visual-Motor Integration**
- **Cutting Skills**
- **Pencil Grip**
- **Eye-Hand Coordination**
- **Hand Strength**

The assessment provide specifics directions and a scoring rubric to determine the child's level. Use the activity matrix on pages 18-19 to match areas of need to the specific activities. The following scoring guide can help identify children most in need. Students falling in the intervention phase of learning should be encouraged to have a Finger Funatics Take-Home Kit for additional practice. See page 74 for more information.

	Scoring Results from Pre- and Post- Assessment		
	100%	80%–90%	73% and lower
	Proficient	Developing	Intervention
Total Points	15/15	14/15 13/15 12/15	11/15 or lower

Visual-Motor Integration Task

Materials needed to complete the assessment:

☐ 10 dried black beans

☐ timer

☐ container with 1-inch opening (e.g., empty medicine or water bottle)

Directions: Have the student put 10 beans in an old medicine or water bottle (1-2 inch opening) as fast as they can. Have them put one bean in at a time. In this task you will be looking for eye-hand coordination and speed.

	Rubric for Scoring		
Score	**Pre-School**	**Kindergarten**	**Grade 1**
1	Student puts 4 or fewer beans in the bottle in 60 seconds.	Student puts 4 or fewer beans in the bottle in 60 seconds.	Student puts 5-10 beans in the bottle in 60 seconds.
2	Student puts 6-7 beans in the bottle in 31-60 seconds.	Student puts 5-10 beans in the bottle in 31-60 seconds.	Student puts 5-10 beans in the bottle in 30 seconds.
3	Student puts 6-7 beans in the bottle in 30 seconds or less.	Student puts 10 beans in the bottle in 30 seconds or less.	Student puts 10 beans in the bottle in less than 15 seconds.

Write any observations in the comments section on the scoring sheet.
Remember to note handedness (R–right , L–left, or B–both).

Cutting

Materials needed to complete the assessment:

☐ blackline master circle on page 81

☐ scissors

Directions: Have the student use a pair of scissors to cut out the circle pattern.
See page 81.

Score	Rubric for Scoring		
	Pre-School	**Kindergarten**	**Grade 1**
1	Student is unable to hold scissors and cut.	Student has difficulty maneuvering the scissors and leaves a ½ inch or greater gap from the cutting line of the circle pattern.	Student cuts raggedly and holds paper incorrectly, but holds scissors correctly.
2	Student is able to snip in to the paper.	Student is able to hold the scissors, but is having difficulty turning the paper correctly. There is a ¼ to ½ inch gap from the cutting line of the circle pattern.	Student's cutting is smoother and closer to the line and holds the paper with thumb on top.
3	Student attempts to cut out the circle.	Student is able to cut out the shapes and maneuvers the paper while cutting around corners. There is ¼ inch or less of a gap from the cutting line of the circle pattern.	Student leaves no gap from cutting line and holds scissors and paper properly.

Write any observations in the comments section on the scoring sheet.
Remember to note handedness (R–right , L–left, or B–both).

Pencil Grip

Materials needed to complete the assessment:

☐ pencil

☐ paper

Directions: Hand the student a pencil at his/her mid-line and note which hand he/she uses. Have the student trace or write their name on a piece of paper. For younger students use a "fat" (size 36) pencil.

	Rubric for Scoring		
Score	**Pre-School**	**Kindergarten**	**Grade 1**
1	Student is unable to hold a pencil or write on the paper.	Student's pencil grip is fisted.	Student takes a few tries to get pencil in correct position.
2	Student's pencil grip is fisted.	Student's pencil grip is an emerging tripod or anything other than a fisted or tripod.	Student uses correct grip inconsistently.
3	Student's pencil grip is an emerging tripod or anything other than fisted or mature tripod.	Student's pencil grip is a mature tripod.	Student can sustain mature tripod grip without fatigue during a task.

	Rubric for Scoring	
Fisted	**Emerging Tripod**	**Mature Tripod**

Write any observations in the comments section on the scoring sheet.
Remember to note handedness (R–right , L–left, or B–both).

Eye-Hand Coordination

Directions: Have the student try to build a tower using ten one-inch wooden cubes. Observe how the student's eyes and hands work together on this task (watch for handedness and block placement to see how their eyes and hands are working together).

	Rubric for Scoring		
Score	**Pre-School**	**Kindergarten**	**Grade 1**
1	Student stacks less than 9 cubes.	Student stacks less than 9 cubes.	Student stacks 9 cubes.
2	Student stacks 9 cubes.	Student stacks 9 cubes.	Student stacks all 10 cubes with one hand.
3	Student stacks all 10 cubes.	Student stacks all 10 cubes.	Student stacks all 10 cubes with both hands alternately.

Write any observations in the comments section on the scoring sheet.

Hand Strength

Materials needed to complete the assessment:

☐ squeeze ball (pre-school)

☐ single hole punch (Kindergarten/Grade 1)

☐ paper

Directions:

Pre-School: Give the student a squeeze ball and have him place it in the palm of the hand. Tell the student to squeeze it as tight as he can and observe.

Kindergarten-Grade 1: Give the student a single hand punch and a piece of scrap paper. Have the student try to punch holes in the paper using the hole punch.

	Rubric for Scoring		
Score	**Pre-School**	**Kindergarten**	**Grade 1**
1	Student is unable to squeeze the ball with much strength.	Student attempts punch a hole in the paper and is unsuccessful.	Student attempts to punch 1-2 holes and struggles.
2	Student can squeeze the ball only about half way.	Student is able to punch 5-7 holes in the paper and struggles easily.	Student is able to punch 10 or more holes and struggles.
3	Student can squeeze the ball with ease in the palm of their hand.	Student is able to punch 20 or more holes in the paper with ease.	Student is able to punch 20-30 holes with ease.

Write any observations in the comments section on the scoring sheet.

Finger Funatics Fine Motor Student Pre- and Post-Assessment

Pre-Assessment Date: _____

Post-Assessment Date: _____

Assessment	Handedness			Rating			Comments
Visual-Motor Integration	L	B	R	1	2	3	
Cutting Skills	L	B	R	1	2	3	
Pencil Grip	L	B	R	1	2	3	
Eye-Hand Coordination	L	B	R	1	2	3	
Hand Strength	L	B	R	1	2	3	

Evaluation Completed by: _____ Date: _____

Total Points: Fall: _____ / 15 (blue) _____ Spring: _____ / 15 (red) _____

- -

Finger Funatics Fine Motor Student Pre- and Post-Assessment

Pre-Assessment Date: _____

Post-Assessment Date: _____

Assessment	Handedness			Rating			Comments
Visual-Motor Integration	L	B	R	1	2	3	
Cutting Skills	L	B	R	1	2	3	
Pencil Grip	L	B	R	1	2	3	
Eye-Hand Coordination	L	B	R	1	2	3	
Hand Strength	L	B	R	1	2	3	

Evaluation Completed by: _____ Date: _____

Total Points: Fall: _____ / 15 (blue) _____ Spring: _____ / 15 (red) _____

Activity
Matrix

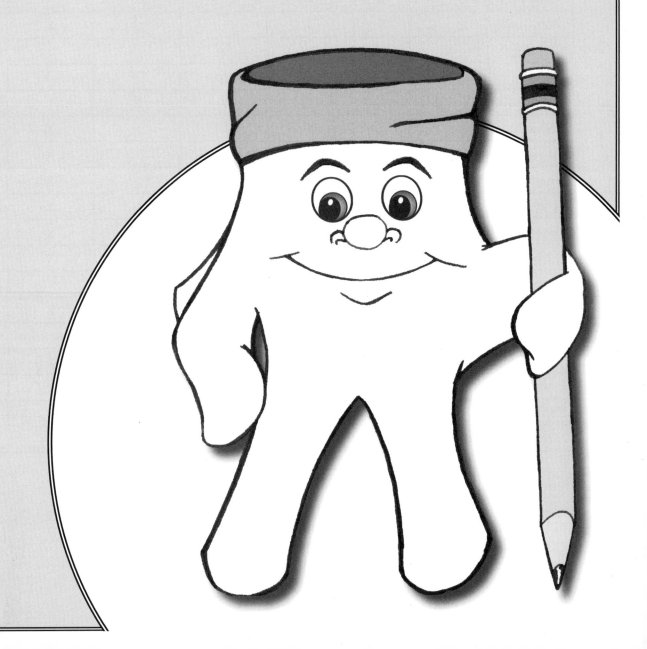

Finger Funatics Activity Matrix

	Activity #	Visual-Motor Integration	Pencil Grip	Cutting Skills	Eye-Hand Coordination	Hand Strength
Treasure Hunt	1		X			X
Funatic-Doh Snip	2		X	X		X
The Button Slide	3					X
Paperclip Point	4					X
Bean Tubs	5					X
Playing Cards	6					X
Clothespin Clamp	7					X
Crazy Lazy 8	8	X				
Pom-Pons Pick-Up	9				X	X
Rubbings	10		X			
Wax Ball	11					X
Number Punch	12		X	X	X	X
Candy Cane Classic	13	X			X	X
Shaving Cream Painting	14	X			X	
Hundred Day Necklace	15	X			X	X
Craft Stick Picture Frame	16				X	X
Sweet Heart	17	X	X	X	X	X
Holiday Punch Card	18	X	X	X	X	X
Funatic-Doh Exercises	19					X
Twisty Pipe Cleaner	20	X			X	X
Penny Grab	21					X
Wreaths	22		X		X	X
Puncture Proof	23				X	X
Symmetric Eggs	24		X	X		X
Clothespin Word Maker	25		X		X	X

	Activity #	Visual-Motor Integration	Pencil Grip	Cutting Skills	Eye-Hand Coordination	Hand Strength
Beans in a Bottle	26	X			X	X
Paperclip Chaining	27				X	X
Sponge Squeeze	28					X
Noodle Lacing	29				X	X
Peg Boards	30	X	X			X
Squeeze Ball Fun	31					X
Barrel of Monkeys™	32	X			X	
Loving to Lace	33	X			X	
Punch Creation	34	X			X	X
Wikki Stix®	35	X				X
Paper Shapers	36	X	X	X	X	X
Stamping	37	X			X	X
Geo-Board Creations	38	X			X	X
Peanut Structure	39				X	X
Perler® Bead Creations	40	X			X	X
Twisty Ties	41				X	X
Pick-Up Sticks	42	X				X
Pix-Os™	43	X			X	X
Punch Crazy	44				X	X
Jumbo Jacks	45				X	X
Link it Up	46				X	X
Dizzy Tops	47				X	X
Mini LITE-BRITE™	48				X	X
Creampuff	49		X		X	X
Squirt!	50				X	X

50 Fine Motor Development Classroom and Home Activities

Developed by Shannon Samulski

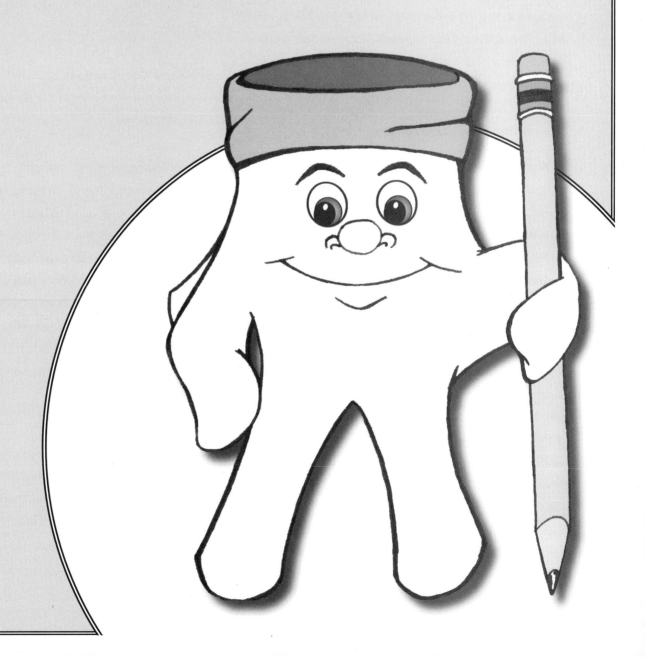

50 Fine Motor Development Classroom and Home Activities

Fine Motor Development

Pre-school, Kindergarten, and Grade 1 students can benefit from experiences that support the development of fine motor skills in the hands and fingers. Children should have strength and dexterity in their hands and fingers before being asked to manipulate a pencil on paper. Working on dexterity and strength first can prevent the development of an inappropriate pencil grip. This is becoming more common as young children are engaged in writing experiences before their hands are ready. The activities will support children's fine motor development and will help to build the strength and dexterity necessary to hold a pencil appropriately.

Areas of Fine Motor Development

Visual-Motor Integration: Visual-Motor integration is the ability of the eyes and hands to work together in smooth efficient patterns. This involves eye-hand coordination and visual perception. Visual-Motor integration is when all systems are working together. This process enables the child to see something, then use their hands and fingers to manipulate it with growing control, accuracy and coordination.

Pencil Grip: Children use many types of pencil grips depending on their fine motor development. In a fisted grip, the pencil is held in a fisted hand with the point of the pencil on the fifth finger side of the hand, which would be typical of very young children. An emergent tripod is a grip that is not mature or fisted (five finger grasp, thumb tucked or wrapped, or wrist flexed or hooked). In a mature tripod, the pencil is held with the tip of the thumb and index finger and rests against the

side of the third finger. The thumb and index finger form a circle.

Cutting Skills: When scissors are held correctly and when they fit a child's hand well, cutting activities will exercise the same muscles that are needed to manipulate a pencil in a mature tripod grip. The correct scissor position is with the thumb and middle finger in the handles of the scissors, the index finger on the outside of the handle to stabilize, with fingers four and five curled into the palm.

Eye-Hand Coordination: Eye-hand coordination is the ability for the eye to guide the hands for near-point activities at tabletop.

Hand Strength: Hand strength is the ability to give force when gripping or grasping an object. Hand strength can not be developed until a child has developed shoulder and upper arm strength. In order to build hand strength, a child needs to perform weight-bearing activities such as lifting a laundry basket, helping carry groceries or carrying bins of books. Once a child develops hand strength he will in turn develop palm strength, which will help him sustain writing tasks for longer. Hand strength is referred to as grasp (pincher) and grip.

Activity Cards

The activity cards found on pages 23-72 can be copied back-to-back on card stock, cut in half and laminated for repeated use. These cards can be sent home in the Finger Funatics Take-Home Kits and used in activity centers.

1 | Treasure Hunt

Areas of Fine-Motor Development	
	Visual-Motor Integration
X	Pencil Grip
	Cutting Skills
	Eye-Hand Coordination
X	Hand Strength

Materials Needed:

☐ approximately 2 oz. of any flavor "Funatic-Doh"
(see recipe on page 77)

☐ small beads (pea-sized or smaller)—10 beads per student

Directions:

1. Have the students hide the 10 beads in the Funatic-Doh.

2. Next, have them squeeze the Funatic-Doh into a ball.

3. Ask them to flatten the Funatic-Doh to find the beads using both hands.

4. Have them hide the beads again in the Funatic-Doh.

5. Repeat using only the right hand, then only the left hand to find the beads. Have them place the opposite hand behind their backs to ensure they are using just one hand.

---

2 | Funatic-Doh Snip

Areas of Fine-Motor Development	
	Visual-Motor Integration
X	Pencil Grip
X	Cutting Skills
	Eye-Hand Coordination
X	Hand Strength

Materials Needed:

☐ approximately 2 oz. of any flavor "Funatic-Doh"
(see recipe on page 77)

☐ scissors

Directions:

1. Have the students roll out their Funatic-Doh on the table to make a worm (in about the diameter and length of a pencil).

2. Next, have them use scissors to cut pieces of Funatic-Doh off the worm.

3. Then have them cut these smaller pieces again, in half, thirds, or fourths.

★ **For more of a challenge:** Have the students roll the Funatic-Doh into a thicker size worm (diameter of a hotdog), which will require more hand strength to cut through.

Finger Funatics
Activity Card

Fine Motor Development Program

www.fingerfunatics.com

© Shannon Samulski, 2010

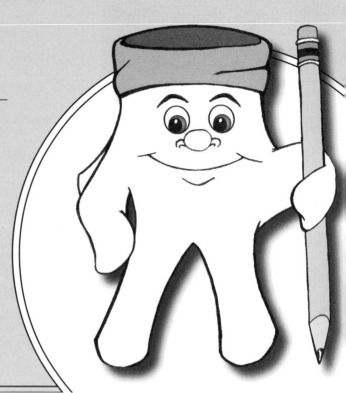

Finger Funatics
Activity Card

Fine Motor Development Program

www.fingerfunatics.com

© Shannon Samulski, 2010

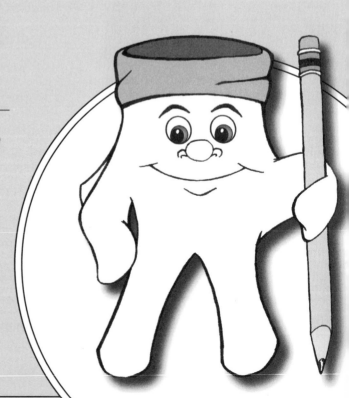

3 The Button Slide

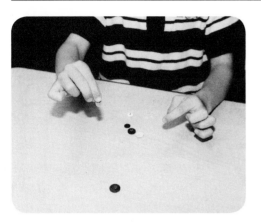

Areas of Fine-Motor Development

	Visual-Motor Integration
	Pencil Grip
	Cutting Skills
	Eye-Hand Coordination
X	Hand Strength *(hand manipulation)*

▦ Materials Needed:

- ☐ small margarine tub (with a slot cut out of the lid)
- ☐ buttons (different shapes and sizes)

▦ Directions:

1. Have the students open the container and remove buttons.
2. Next, have them place the buttons on table, some on one side of the container and the rest on the other.
3. Have them practice picking up the buttons with only the thumb and pointer finger (right for buttons on the right side of the container and left for the buttons on the left side of the container). Challenge them to not use the edge of the table or both hands to pick up buttons.
4. Still using one hand, have them place the button into the slot in the lid of the container.
5. Encourage them to try the same sequence using thumb/middle finger, thumb/ring finger, and thumb/pinky with each hand.

4 Paperclip Point

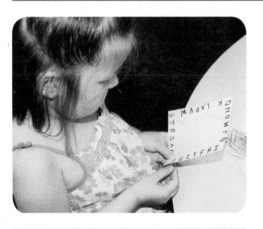

Areas of Fine-Motor Development

	Visual-Motor Integration
	Pencil Grip
	Cutting Skills
	Eye-Hand Coordination
X	Hand Strength *(finger manipulation)*

▦ Materials Needed:

- ☐ ABC/number border cards *(see pages 83-84)*
  These cards can be copied back-to-back on card stock, cut in half and laminated for repeated use.
- ☐ several large and small paperclips

▦ Directions:

1. Pass out an ABC/number border card and a pile of paperclips.
2. Have the student's use the number border side and place a paperclip on the numeral 1 and then continue putting paper clips in number order.
3. Next, have them flip over their cards to the ABC border and have them clip the letters in alphabetical order.
4. Have students spell their names or sight words by putting paperclips on the appropriate letters.

★ **For more of a challenge,** have the students use the smaller paperclips to complete the same activity.

Finger Funatics
Activity Card

Fine Motor Development Program

www.fingerfunatics.com

© Shannon Samulski, 2010

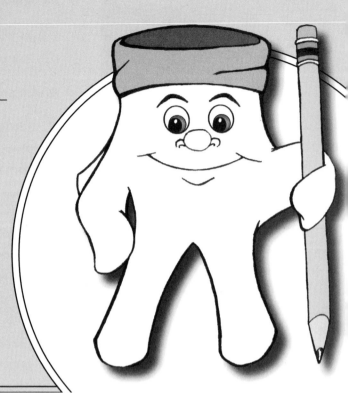

Finger Funatics
Activity Card

Fine Motor Development Program

www.fingerfunatics.com

© Shannon Samulski, 2010

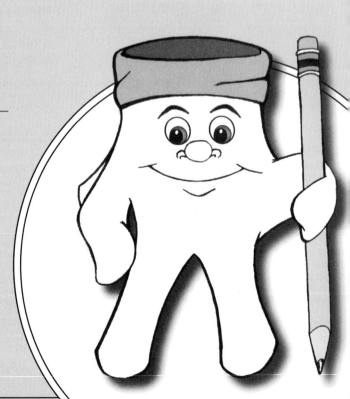

5 Bean Tubs

Materials Needed:

☐ small margarine tub or plastic storage container

☐ assorted dried beans (kidney, pinto, etc.)

Directions:

1. Dump beans out of the tub onto a table. Have the student use only two fingers at a time to pick up beans and then place them at the bottom of the tub. Start with the pincher fingers (pointer and thumb) and then have students use their thumb and middle finger, thumb and ring finger, then thumb and pinky.

2. They can sort the beans by size, color, or shape.

3. Be sure students don't drag the bean to the end of the table to pick up. They should use only two fingers to pinch and pick up beans.

Areas of Fine-Motor Development	
	Visual-Motor Integration
	Pencil Grip
	Cutting Skills
	Eye-Hand Coordination
X	Hand Strength *(pincher grasp)*

---

6 Playing Cards

Materials Needed:

☐ 6-8 playing cards, any type

Directions:

1. Lay out six to eight cards and have the students practice turning them over without dragging or sliding the card to the end of the table (this can be tough for many children because they tend to bend the cards).

2. Students can turn over every other card, turn the cards side-ways then straight (any variation of grasping the cards is fine).

★ **For more of a challenge,** time students to see who can do it properly the fastest.

Areas of Fine-Motor Development	
	Visual-Motor Integration
	Pencil Grip
	Cutting Skills
	Eye-Hand Coordination
X	Hand Strength *(grasp)*

Finger Funatics
Activity Card

Fine Motor Development Program

www.fingerfunatics.com

© Shannon Samulski, 2010

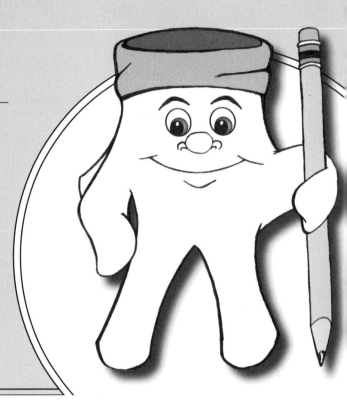

Finger Funatics
Activity Card

Fine Motor Development Program

www.fingerfunatics.com

© Shannon Samulski, 2010

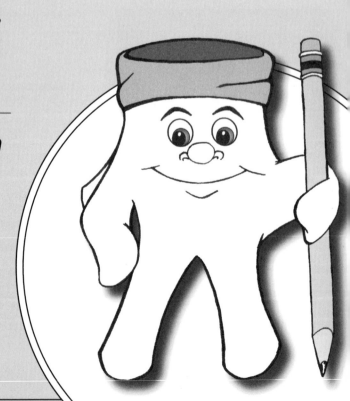

7 Clothespin Clamp

Materials Needed:

- [ ] clothespins (spring type)
- [ ] margarine tub or plastic storage container
- [ ] playing cards

Directions:

1. Students can practice pinching clothespins open and closed starting with their pincher fingers and then trying other fingers (using only two at a time).

2. Once they are able to open and close with some ease they can try to pin several clothespins on the rim of a margarine or plastic storage container, around a playing card, on their clothes, or on any thin surface.

3. Putting clothespins on and off of things will use the pincher motion, which will help strengthen those small muscles.

	Areas of Fine-Motor Development
	Visual-Motor Integration
	Pencil Grip
	Cutting Skills
	Eye-Hand Coordination
X	Hand Strength *(pincher grasp)*

8 Crazy Lazy 8

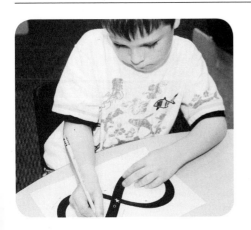

Materials Needed:

- [ ] Lazy 8 figure on page 82 (blackline master)
- [ ] pencil
- [ ] dry erase markers
- [ ] eraser

Directions:

1. Copy the Lazy 8 pattern for each student.

2. Have them turn the Lazy 8 pattern on its side. Next have the students trace the Lazy 8 pattern over and over again. They will start in the middle at the star and follow the arrow directions on the thick black Lazy 8 line. Have them complete this same route over and over again.

3. Make sure they are following the line direction with their eyes as they trace.

4. You can laminate the Lazy 8 pattern for repeated use and have students trace the lines with dry erase markers. The students can then erase their dry erase marker in the same pattern using the eraser.

	Areas of Fine-Motor Development
X	Visual-Motor Integration
	Pencil Grip
	Cutting Skills
	Eye-Hand Coordination
	Hand Strength

Finger Funatics
Activity Card

Fine Motor Development Program

www.fingerfunatics.com

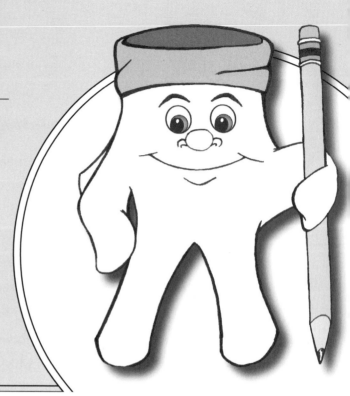

Finger Funatics
Activity Card

Fine Motor Development Program

www.fingerfunatics.com

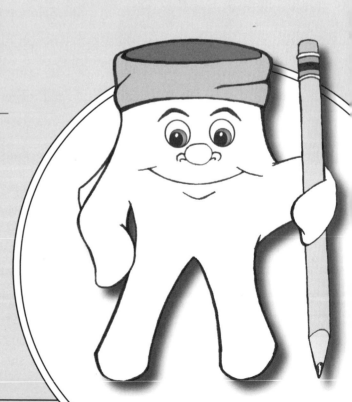

9 Pom-Pons Pick-Up

Materials Needed:

- ☐ clothespins (spring type)
- ☐ bag of pom-pons or cotton balls
- ☐ small margarine containers

Directions:

1. Set the students up in teams and give them each a clothespin to use as their tool in this task.

2. Place a pile of pom-pons and a container in the center of their table.

3. Tell the students to try to get as many pom-pons in the container as they can. They can use ONLY their clothes pins as tools (not their fingers).

★ **For more of a challenge,** have students see how fast they can complete this task.

Areas of Fine-Motor Development	
	Visual-Motor Integration
	Pencil Grip
	Cutting Skills
X	Eye-Hand Coordination
X	Hand Strength (pincher grasp)

10 Rubbings

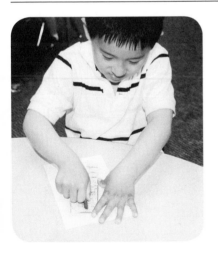

Materials Needed:

- ☐ variety of stencils (animals, letters, shapes, etc.)
- ☐ crayons
- ☐ paper

Directions:

1. Ask students to peel a variety of crayons.

2. Show students how to take the crayon and hold it sideways using 3 or 4 fingers (demonstrate how to do this as it is not how you normally hold a crayon).

3. Take a stencil and put it under the paper, and have students rub over the paper covering the stencil.

4. They will need to hold the paper and stencil in place with one hand while rubbing with the other.

Note: Larger pre-school crayons might make this activity easier for some students.

Areas of Fine-Motor Development	
	Visual-Motor Integration
X	Pencil Grip
	Cutting Skills
	Eye-Hand Coordination
	Hand Strength

Finger Funatics
Activity Card

Fine Motor Development Program

www.fingerfunatics.com

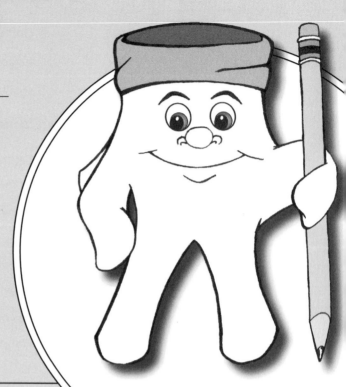

Finger Funatics
Activity Card

Fine Motor Development Program

www.fingerfunatics.com

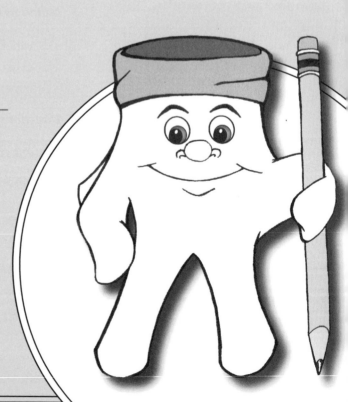

11 Wax Ball

Materials Needed:

- ☐ four sheets of waxed paper per student
- ☐ plastic tub or bucket

Directions:

1. Place four sheets of waxed paper on the table.

2. Have students place the palm of one hand on the table with finger tips touching the edge of the paper.

3. Keeping their wrist on the table, have the students crumble the paper into their palms.

4. Next have students toss their balls of waxed paper in to a plastic tub or bucket.

5. Then remove the ball of waxed paper and spread it flat on the table using only one hand and finger tips, keeping wrists on the table.

	Areas of Fine-Motor Development
	Visual-Motor Integration
	Pencil Grip
	Cutting Skills
	Eye-Hand Coordination
X	Hand Strength

12 Number Punch

Materials Needed:

- ☐ single hole punch
- ☐ large construction paper divided into 10 equal sections, each labeled with numerals 1-20 (1-10 on one side, and 11-20 on the other, see photo)
- ☐ multi-colored construction paper scraps
- ☐ glue or glue sticks
- ☐ optional: for younger students, use Cheerios®, Kix® cereal, beans, etc.

Directions:

1. Demonstrate how to use the paper punch using the scrap construction paper.

2. Have the students glue on the appropriate number of punched out circles for each number. For example the number 5 will have 5 circle punches glued down (or Cheerios®, beans, etc.).

3. If gluing becomes too frustrating, they can just place the correct number of punches or cereal on the appropriate number.

4. Once they have completed numbers 1-10, have them turn the paper over and repeat the activity for numbers 11-20.

	Areas of Fine-Motor Development
	Visual-Motor Integration
X	Pencil Grip
X	Cutting Skills
X	Eye-Hand Coordination
X	Hand Strength *(pincher grasp)*

Finger Funatics
Activity Card

Fine Motor Development Program

www.fingerfunatics.com

© Shannon Samulski, 2010

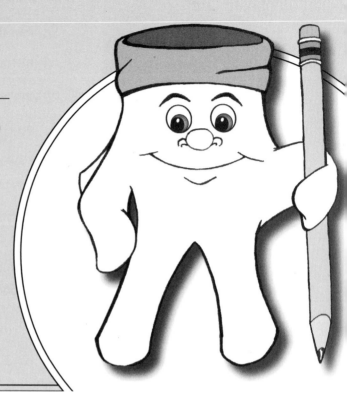

Finger Funatics
Activity Card

Fine Motor Development Program

www.fingerfunatics.com

© Shannon Samulski, 2010

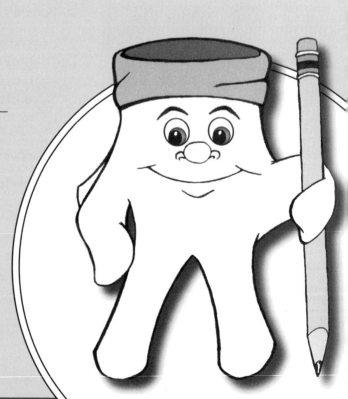

13 Candy Cane Classic

Materials Needed:

- ☐ bucket of red beads
- ☐ bucket of white beads
- ☐ class set of pipe cleaners (cut in half)
- ☐ a few spools of red ribbon

Directions:

1. Each student will get a half of a pipe cleaner and several red and white beads.

2. Students will need to bend and pinch one end of the pipe cleaner and then begin threading the beads in a red and white pattern onto the pipe cleaner.

3. Once they have filled up the pipe cleaner, they will pinch the other end of the candy cane and curve it to make the shape of a candy cane.

4. When students are finished an adult can help them tie on the red ribbon to create a candy cane classic gift to hang at home.

	Areas of Fine-Motor Development
X	Visual-Motor Integration
	Pencil Grip
	Cutting Skills
X	Eye-Hand Coordination
X	Hand Strength

14 Shaving Cream Painting

Materials Needed:

- ☐ shaving cream or gel

Directions:

1. Have the students sit at a table or desk. (They need a large enough area for them to work with the shaving cream).

2. Squirt shaving cream on their area and have the students spread it out (be sure they have enough to be able to see what they are writing).

3. They can practice writing their numbers, letters, names, color words, and sight words in the shaving cream.

4. Have them try to do the Lazy 8 pattern in the shaving cream following the sequence (starting in the middle, going up to the right, around, cross the middle and go up to the left and around).

5. When students are finished, wipe away the shaving cream, leaving clean and disinfected tables!

	Areas of Fine-Motor Development
X	Visual-Motor Integration
	Pencil Grip
	Cutting Skills
X	Eye-Hand Coordination
	Hand Strength

Finger Funatics
Activity Card

Fine Motor Development Program

www.fingerfunatics.com

© Shannon Samulski, 2010

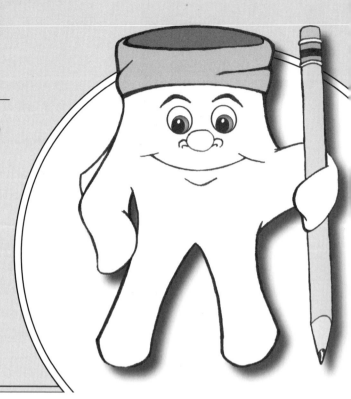

Finger Funatics
Activity Card

Fine Motor Development Program

www.fingerfunatics.com

© Shannon Samulski, 2010

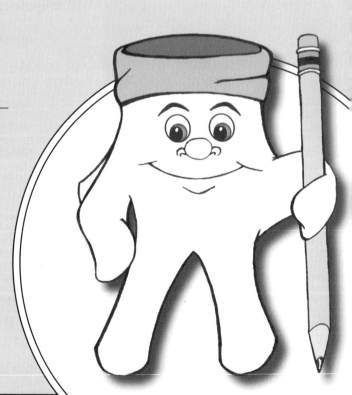

15 Hundred Day Necklace

Materials Needed:

☐ Cheerios® cereal
☐ Fruit Loops® cereal
☐ string or yarn

Directions:

1. This activity can be used to celebrate the 100th day of school (or for families, the 100th day of the year).

2. Give each student a long string with a large knot tied at the end to prevent the cereal from falling off.

3. Have the students string 10 Fruit Loops at a time onto a string to make their necklace. In between each set of ten have them lace in 1 Cheerio to denote each group of 10. Younger students can work in partners or table groups.

4. Other options: Students can sort the Fruit Loops® and make one set of 10 all green, another all red, etc. Or they could do a set of Cheerios® followed by a set of Fruit Loops®. They could also do patterns using the colors of the Fruit Loops® or Cheerios® combined with Fruit Loops®. Let children be creative.

5. Once they have finished, tie off the end, then tie ends together to make a loop. They can wear it on the 100th day of school.

Areas of Fine-Motor Development	
X	Visual-Motor Integration
	Pencil Grip
	Cutting Skills
X	Eye-Hand Coordination
X	Hand Strength (pincher grasp)

16 Craft Stick Picture Frame

Materials Needed:

☐ large craft sticks
☐ glue
☐ glitter, buttons, beads, jewels, beans, etc.
☐ card stock or cardboard

Directions:

1. Give each student four large craft sticks and have them glue them together in a square to make a frame.

2. Next, using glue have them decorate each of the sticks by gluing on glitter, buttons, beads, jewels, beans etc. Challenge them to completely hide the craft stick so each area is covered.

3. Encourage the students to use their pincher grasp (pointer and thumb) to place the items on the sticks.

4. Have them put a picture on the card stock, and glue it to the back of the frame.

Areas of Fine-Motor Development	
	Visual-Motor Integration
	Pencil Grip
	Cutting Skills
X	Eye-Hand Coordination
X	Hand Strength

Finger Funatics
Activity Card

Fine Motor Development Program

www.fingerfunatics.com

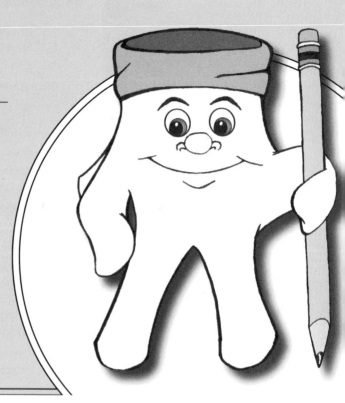

Finger Funatics
Activity Card

Fine Motor Development Program

www.fingerfunatics.com

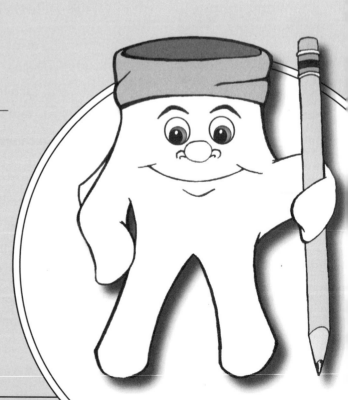

17 Sweet Heart

Materials Needed:

- [ ] red, white, pink, or purple construction paper
- [ ] yarn
- [ ] scissors
- [ ] single paper punch

Directions:

1. Each student will trace and cut out a large heart out of construction paper (you can make a pattern for them to trace to make it easier).

2. Have the student punch holes around the perimeter of the heart.

3. Next, help them tie their string in one of the holes, so they can begin lacing their hearts. They could do outside loops or thread it through each hole (up through the back and back down through the front).

4. When they have finished they can decorate their heart for Valentine's Day.

Areas of Fine-Motor Development	
X	Visual-Motor Integration
X	Pencil Grip
X	Cutting Skills
X	Eye-Hand Coordination
X	Hand Strength

18 Holiday Card Punch

Materials Needed:

- [ ] old holiday cards
- [ ] shoelace or yarn
- [ ] single card punch

Directions:

1. Have students choose an old holiday card.

2. Have them punch holes around the perimeter of the card.

3. Next, tie a knot at one end of a shoe lace or yarn and lace it through the different holes.

4. They can loop the lace or feed it through the holes up and down.

Areas of Fine-Motor Development	
X	Visual-Motor Integration
X	Pencil Grip
X	Cutting Skills
X	Eye-Hand Coordination
X	Hand Strength (pincher grasp)

Finger Funatics
Activity Card

Fine Motor Development Program

www.fingerfunatics.com

Finger Funatics
Activity Card

Fine Motor Development Program

www.fingerfunatics.com

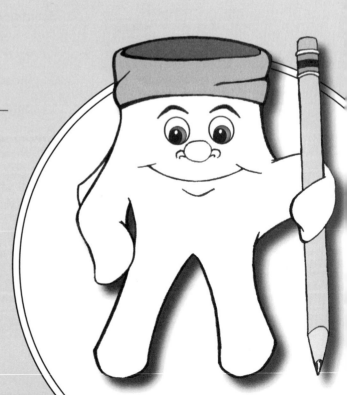

19 Funatic-Doh Exercises

Materials Needed:

☐ approximately 2 oz. of any flavor "Funatic-Doh" *(see recipe on page 77)*—one for each student

Directions:

1. Demonstrate the exercises below, then, have students copy you. Give ample time to practice before moving onto another exercise.

2. Squeeze and release the dough ball by holding it palm up. Repeat with other hand.

3. Roll the dough ball between both hands with one palm up and one palm down.

4. Roll the dough ball around and around on the table with one hand, saying "round and round".

5. Flatten the dough ball by pounding it with the side of a fist. Try the other fist.

6. Flatten the dough ball with the side of an open hand. Try the other hand.

7. Form a mountain by placing hand over flattened dough slowly closing it.

8. Using thumb and forefinger of one hand pinch off small pieces of the ball, then dab back together.

9. Flatten the ball by pounding it with the palm of an open hand. Say, "You're making it so flat."

Areas of Fine-Motor Development	
	Visual-Motor Integration
	Pencil Grip
	Cutting Skills
	Eye-Hand Coordination
X	Hand Strength

20 Twisty Pipe Cleaner

Materials Needed:

☐ variety of pipe cleaners

☐ pencil

☐ noodles (penne)

☐ optional: twist ties

Directions:

1. Have the students lay the pipe cleaner flat on the table and then twist it around in a circle like a snail.

2. Try to uncoil the pipe cleaner with one hand for a challenge.

3. Make shapes or letters with the pipe cleaners.

4. Wrap pipe cleaners around a pencil.

5. Twist two halves of the pipe cleaner together, then untwist.

6. Thread noodles on to pipe cleaner or twist ties.

Areas of Fine-Motor Development	
X	Visual-Motor Integration
	Pencil Grip
	Cutting Skills
X	Eye-Hand Coordination
X	Hand Strength

Finger Funatics
Activity Card

Fine Motor Development Program

www.fingerfunatics.com

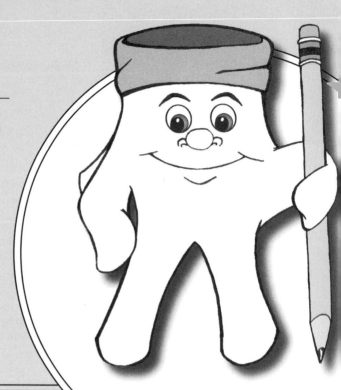

Finger Funatics
Activity Card

Fine Motor Development Program

www.fingerfunatics.com

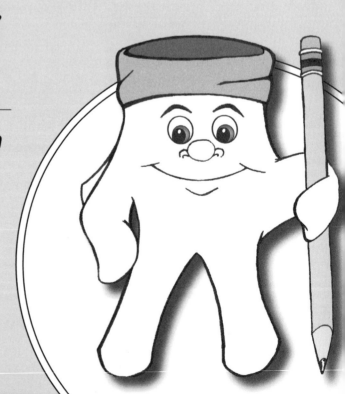

21 *Penny Grab*

Materials Needed:

- ☐ 10–20 pennies
- ☐ small paper cups
- ☐ bingo chips

Directions:

1. Have the students place all their pennies on the table and spread them out.

2. Have them pick up one at a time without sliding the coin to the edge of the table.

3. To make the task more difficult have students try not using their fingertips while picking up the pennies. Instead, have them round their palms to grasp the coin.

4. Have them try to pick up a penny using different finger combinations, but without sliding the penny.

5. You can also use bingo chips and sort by color to add more fun to the task.

	Areas of Fine-Motor Development
	Visual-Motor Integration
	Pencil Grip
	Cutting Skills
	Eye-Hand Coordination
X	**Hand Strength** *(manipulation)*

22 *Wreaths*

Materials Needed:

- ☐ green tissue paper
- ☐ paper plates
- ☐ glue
- ☐ scissors
- ☐ pencil

Directions:

1. Each student will take a paper plate and fold it in half lightly. Cut out the center portion of the paper plate to make a wreath (Pre-school and Kindergarten students will need assistance).

2. Next the students will crumble small pieces of green tissue paper and glue each piece to the wreath. Older students can wrap the tissue paper around a pencil eraser, dip in glue, and place on the paper plate to make the wreath.

3. Continue until the entire paper plate is covered.

	Areas of Fine-Motor Development
	Visual-Motor Integration
	Pencil Grip
	Cutting Skills
	Eye-Hand Coordination
X	**Hand Strength** *(manipulation)*

Finger Funatics
Activity Card

Fine Motor Development Program

www.fingerfunatics.com

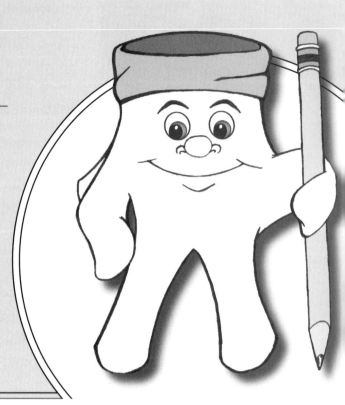

Finger Funatics
Activity Card

Fine Motor Development Program

www.fingerfunatics.com

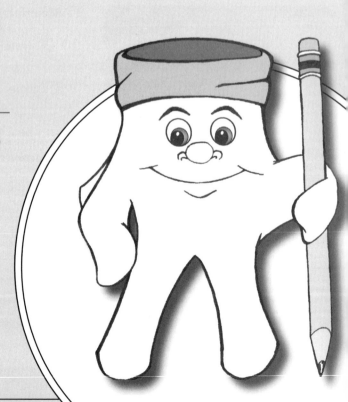

23 Puncture Proof

Areas of Fine-Motor Development	
	Visual-Motor Integration
	Pencil Grip
	Cutting Skills
X	Eye-Hand Coordination
X	Hand Strength

Materials Needed:

- ☐ thumb tacks
- ☐ foam paper, Styrofoam™ lunch tray or plate
- ☐ word/picture/name templates
  (to be laid over foam paper as a guide)

Directions:

1. Demonstrate how to hold a template over the foam paper and how to hold the thumb tack.

2. Have students use the thumb tacks to punch out letters of their names in the foam by punching along the outline of the letters.

3. Students can also punch out dotted pictures into the foam.

4. Students can complete this same process to punch out basic sight words.

5. This activity may not be appropriate for pre-school students.

---

24 Symmetric Eggs

Areas of Fine-Motor Development	
	Visual-Motor Integration
X	Pencil Grip
X	Cutting Skills
	Eye-Hand Coordination
X	Hand Strength

Materials Needed:

- ☐ white construction paper
- ☐ egg template on card stock for students to trace
- ☐ glitter and glue or glitter glue sticks
- ☐ scissors
- ☐ pencil

Directions:

1. Have each student trace the egg template on white construction paper.

2. Next have them cut out their traced egg and fold it exactly in half vertically.

3. Open up the fold and lay the egg flat.

4. Using the glue have students create a design on one side of the fold line, and then refold and reopen. Then, sprinkle glitter on the glue (if you are using glitter glue sticks they can just draw their design). The design will appear on both sides of the egg.

Finger Funatics
Activity Card

Fine Motor Development Program

www.fingerfunatics.com

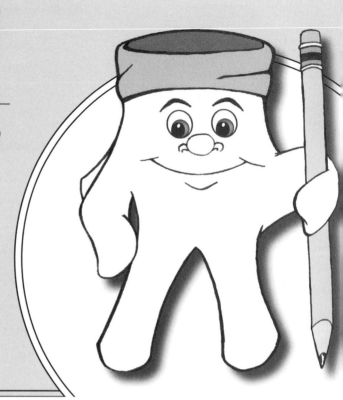

Finger Funatics
Activity Card

Fine Motor Development Program

www.fingerfunatics.com

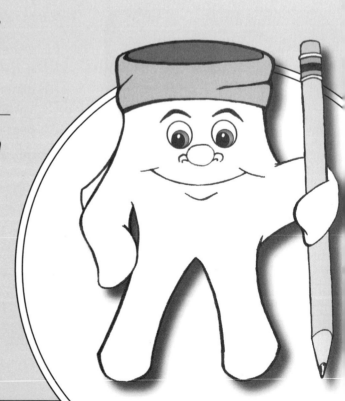

25 Clothespin Word Marker

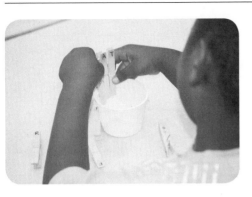

Materials Needed:

- ☐ clothespins (spring type), each marked with a different letter written at the top
- ☐ card stock or small margarine containers

Directions:

1. Lay out several clothespins with letters written at the top of the clothespin.
2. Give each student a sheet of card stock or a small margarine container.
3. Have the student use the clothespin letters to create words (sight words, color words, names, etc.) by clamping each clothespin to the card stock or margarine container.
4. After students have made a word they can write their word on the paper; create a list of words they made with the clothespins.
5. For younger students put uppercase letters out of order on the card stock and write lowercase letters on the clothespins. The student can work on clamping the lowercase letters to the correct uppercase letter.

Areas of Fine-Motor Development	
	Visual-Motor Integration
X	Pencil Grip
	Cutting Skills
X	Eye-Hand Coordination
X	Hand Strength *(pincher grasp)*

26 Beans in a Bottle

Materials Needed:

- ☐ water bottle with an "X" cut in the top of the bottle **OR**
- ☐ a quart- or pint-sized milk carton with a screw top (such as Half & Half creamer carton) with an "X" cut on one side of the carton
- ☐ 10 dry beans (black, pinto, etc.)
- ☐ tweezers (optional)

Directions:

1. Have the student take the lid off the bottle and pour the beans onto the table or floor.
2. Then have them put the beans back in the bottle by pushing one bean at a time through the "X" at the top of the bottle. (For a more advanced skill have students use tweezers to place the beans in the opening of the bottle).

Areas of Fine-Motor Development	
	Visual-Motor Integration
X	Pencil Grip
X	Cutting Skills
	Eye-Hand Coordination
X	Hand Strength

Finger Funatics
Activity Card

Fine Motor Development Program

www.fingerfunatics.com

© Shannon Samulski, 2010

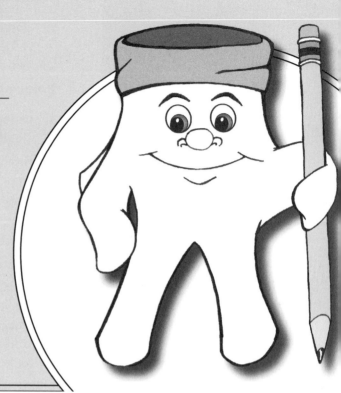

Finger Funatics
Activity Card

Fine Motor Development Program

www.fingerfunatics.com

© Shannon Samulski, 2010

27 Paperclip Chaining

Materials Needed:

☐ bin of large and small paperclips

Directions:

1. Use the large paperclips for students with weaker hand strength and the small paperclips with more advanced students.

2. Have them make a paperclip chain by hooking one paperclip into another. See how many paperclips it takes to make a chain as long as your hand, arm, or foot.

3. Once they have completed their chains, have them work to take apart the paperclips. This can be difficult for some students depending on their hand strength.

Areas of Fine-Motor Development	
	Visual-Motor Integration
	Pencil Grip
	Cutting Skills
	Eye-Hand Coordination
X	Hand Strength (finger manipulation)

28 Sponge Squeeze

Materials Needed:

☐ several small tubs filled with water

☐ bucket of sponges

Directions:

1. Pair up students into teams of two or three. Give each team one empty tub, one tub filled with water and a sponge for each team member.

2. Have students dip their sponge in the water and then squeeze out the water out into the empty tub.

3. Let them continue until all of the water has been squeezed out of one tub and into the other.

4. Once the students understand the activity you can have a contest to see which team can empty its tub the fastest.

Areas of Fine-Motor Development	
	Visual-Motor Integration
	Pencil Grip
X	Cutting Skills
	Eye-Hand Coordination
X	Hand Strength

Finger Funatics
Activity Card

Fine Motor Development Program

www.fingerfunatics.com

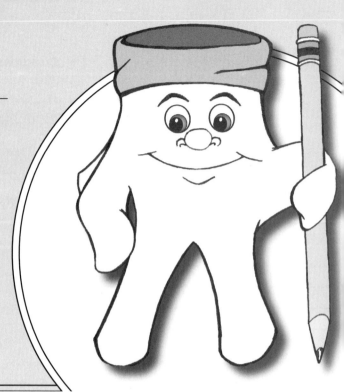

Finger Funatics
Activity Card

Fine Motor Development Program

www.fingerfunatics.com

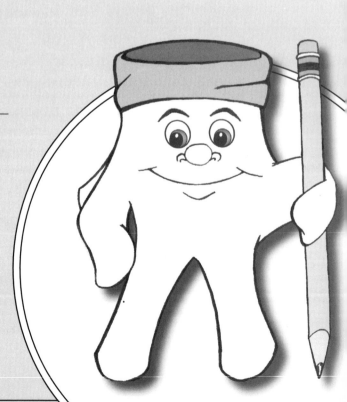

29 Noodle Lacing

Materials Needed:

- ☐ markers
- ☐ box of noodles (penne type, long with a hole big enough to string)
- ☐ shoelace, yarn, or ribbon

Directions:

1. Have students lace the noodles onto a shoelace or yarn. Have them hold the noodle with one hand while stringing the shoelace or yarn through the hole.

2. Try using ribbon for more of a challenge. Students will need to wiggle the ribbon to get it to slide through the noodle.

3. Students can hold the noodles in one hand loosely and color the noodles with markers (be sure they don't hold it too tightly or the noodle will break). They can then pattern, sort or count the noodles.

Areas of Fine-Motor Development	
X	Visual-Motor Integration
	Pencil Grip
	Cutting Skills
X	Eye-Hand Coordination
	Hand Strength

30 Pegboards

Materials Needed:

- ☐ class set of pegboards
- ☐ buckets of multi-colored pegs

Directions:

1. Pass out one pegboard per student, and place a small dish of pegs in front of each student.

2. Let the students practice using index finger and thumb to place pegs in holes on the pegboard.

3. Have them form shapes such as a triangles, squares, and circles.

4. They can sort the pegs by color, then line up the same color in each row and arrange the rows from smallest to largest.

5. They can try to make a pattern of pegs and repeat the pattern going around the perimeter of the board until they run out of the correct colors (patterns such as ABAB, AABB, ABC, etc).

6. Start a sample pattern for the students to continue independently.

★ **For more of a challenge,** have the students put in the pegs using different finger combinations.

Areas of Fine-Motor Development	
X	Visual-Motor Integration
X	Pencil Grip
	Cutting Skills
X	Eye-Hand Coordination
	Hand Strength

Finger Funatics
Activity Card

Fine Motor Development Program

www.fingerfunatics.com

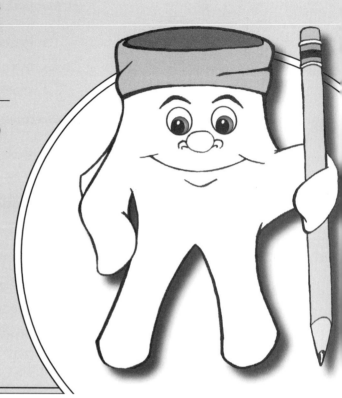

© Shannon Samulski, 2010

Finger Funatics
Activity Card

Fine Motor Development Program

www.fingerfunatics.com

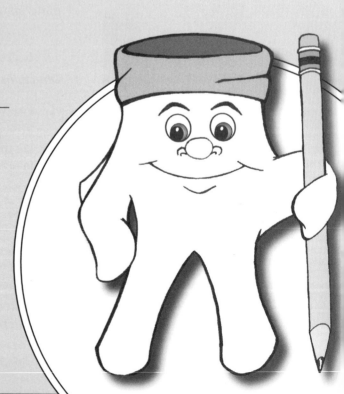

© Shannon Samulski, 2010

31 Squeeze Ball Fun!

Materials Needed:

☐ class set of squeeze balls

Directions:

1. The students will each receive a squeeze ball.

2. Ask the students to squeeze the ball with their right hand pumping ten times.

3. Switch hands and repeat.

4. Place ball between thumb and index finger and squeeze ten times

5. Exercises can be repeated using different two-finger combinations.

6. Try spider bites by putting finger tips on the ball and squeezing (see photo above).

Areas of Fine-Motor Development	
	Visual-Motor Integration
	Pencil Grip
	Cutting Skills
	Eye-Hand Coordination
X	Hand Strength

32 Barrel of Monkeys™

Materials Needed:

☐ set of Barrel of Monkeys™—enough for two students to share a barrel

Directions:

1. Put the students in groups of two or three and give each group one Barrel of Monkeys™.

2. Demonstrate how the game works first.

3. Have the first student shake the Barrel of Monkeys™ and spill it out on the table or floor.

4. The first student picks up one monkey and tries to link as many monkeys as possible without dropping any monkeys.

5. Remind them they can use only one hand to do this activity.

6. When a student drops a monkey, it is the next student's turn to play.

Areas of Fine-Motor Development	
X	Visual-Motor Integration
	Pencil Grip
	Cutting Skills
X	Eye-Hand Coordination
	Hand Strength

Finger Funatics
Activity Card

Fine Motor Development Program

www.fingerfunatics.com

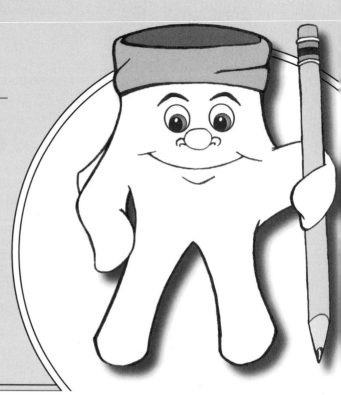

Finger Funatics
Activity Card

Fine Motor Development Program

www.fingerfunatics.com

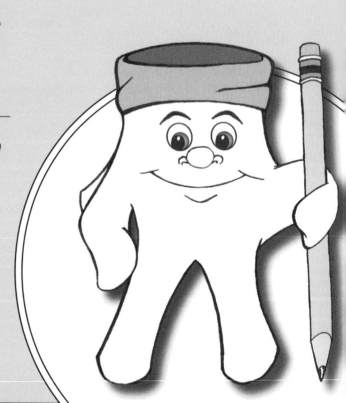

33 Loving to Lace

Materials Needed:

☐ boxes of alphabet, number, animal, or shaped lacing cards

☐ string

Directions:

1. Pass out a lacing card to each student.

2. Demonstrate to the class how to lace the cards by sewing in and out of the holes.

3. Have the students start to lace their cards using the string that is attached to their symbol.

Areas of Fine-Motor Development	
X	Visual-Motor Integration
	Pencil Grip
	Cutting Skills
X	Eye-Hand Coordination
	Hand Strength

34 Punch Creation

Materials Needed:

☐ bin of giant and small shape punches (star, heart, snowflake, hand, foot, etc.)

☐ hand punches (tears, dragonfly, square, triangle, etc.)

☐ white construction paper (one piece for each student)

☐ multi-colored construction paper scraps

☐ glue or glue sticks

Directions:

1. Pass out one sheet of white construction paper to each student. In the middle of each table place three to five punches in the center with multi-colored construction paper scraps.

2. Demonstrate how to use the shape punches and the hand punches.

3. Tell the students to punch out several shapes or figures and glue them on their white construction paper to make a picture. The students may rotate the punches from table to table so that all the students get a chance to use all of the punches.

4. Hang up their Punch Creation with their name on it.

Areas of Fine-Motor Development	
X	Visual-Motor Integration
	Pencil Grip
	Cutting Skills
X	Eye-Hand Coordination
X	Hand Strength

Finger Funatics
Activity Card

Fine Motor Development Program

www.fingerfunatics.com

© Shannon Samulski, 2010

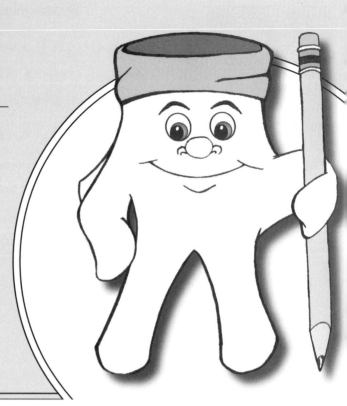

Finger Funatics
Activity Card

Fine Motor Development Program

www.fingerfunatics.com

© Shannon Samulski, 2010

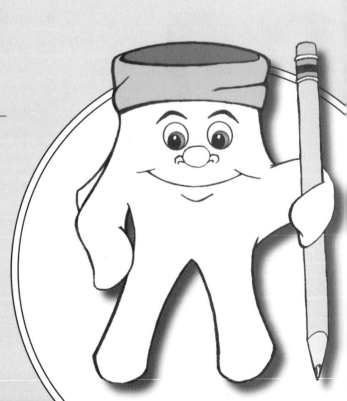

35 *Wikki Stix®*

Materials Needed:

☐ class set of Wikki Stix®

Directions:

1. Give each student several Wikki Stix® and let them play with them for a few minutes.

2. Demonstrate how they bend and twist to make different shapes or figures.

3. Next have students try spelling out their names using a capital for the first letter and lowercase for the rest.

4. You could have them spell out common sight words with two or three letters per word.

Areas of Fine-Motor Development	
X	Visual-Motor Integration
	Pencil Grip
	Cutting Skills
X	Eye-Hand Coordination
	Hand Strength

36 *Paper Shapers™*

Materials Needed:

☐ scrap colored/white paper or magazine pages
☐ 2-3 sets of Paper Shapers™
☐ glue
☐ regular pieces of paper for each student
☐ crayons

Directions:

1. At each table put three to four Paper Shapers™ and scrap paper or magazine pages.

2. Show the students all of the different patterns the Paper Shapers™ can create by cutting out sample borders.

3. Have the students make a border with their paper shaper and glue it to a piece of white paper.

4. Let the students cut cool-edged shapes with their Paper Shapers™ and glue them on their page. (They can use crayons to complete details in their picture if they choose.)

Areas of Fine-Motor Development	
X	Visual-Motor Integration
X	Pencil Grip
X	Cutting Skills
X	Eye-Hand Coordination
X	Hand Strength

Finger Funatics
Activity Card

Fine Motor Development Program

www.fingerfunatics.com

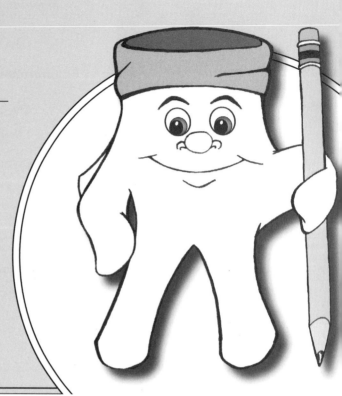

© Shannon Samulski, 2010

Finger Funatics
Activity Card

Fine Motor Development Program

www.fingerfunatics.com

© Shannon Samulski, 2010

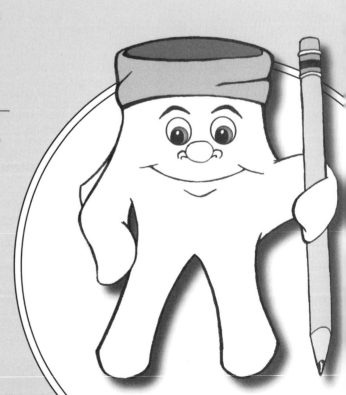

37 Stamping

Materials Needed:

- ☐ clear upper- and lowercase stamps
- ☐ 2-8 packs of multi-colored ink
- ☐ lined paper or squared paper large enough for stamp

Directions:

1. Pass out a piece of lined paper to each student.

2. Select two to three ink pads for each table and divide stamps up among students.

3. Demonstrate how to see if you are on the line when stamping by looking through the clear portion of the stamp before stamping.

4. The students will use letter stamps to stamp out their name, color words, number words, or sight words.

5. Have the students do a known words race—see how many two- to three-letter words they can make with the stamps in a given period of time.

Areas of Fine-Motor Development	
X	Visual-Motor Integration
	Pencil Grip
	Cutting Skills
X	Eye-Hand Coordination
X	Hand Strength

38 Geo-Board Creations

Materials Needed:

- ☐ class set of Geo-Boards
- ☐ container of multi-colored rubber bands

Directions:

1. Give each student a Geo-Board and several rubber bands.

2. Have the students play with the Geo-Boards by attaching rubber bands to make shapes, lines, letters, etc.

3. Once they have played with the Geo-boards awhile demonstrate letters (with straight lines) that you would like to make (M, N, E, F, L, etc.).

4. Have the students make the shape you are making (square, rectangle, triangle, right triangle).

Areas of Fine-Motor Development	
X	Visual-Motor Integration
	Pencil Grip
	Cutting Skills
X	Eye-Hand Coordination
X	Hand Strength *(pincher grasp)*

Finger Funatics
Activity Card

Fine Motor Development Program

www.fingerfunatics.com

© Shannon Samulski, 2010

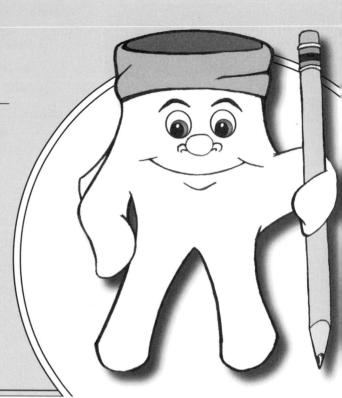

Finger Funatics
Activity Card

Fine Motor Development Program

www.fingerfunatics.com

© Shannon Samulski, 2010

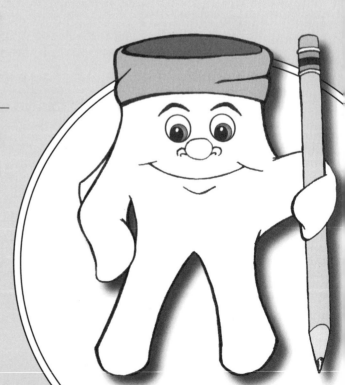

39 Peanut Structure

Materials Needed:

- ☐ packing peanuts or small Styrofoam™ balls
- ☐ toothpicks

Directions:

1. Give each student a pile of packing peanuts and toothpicks.

2. Have students use the toothpicks to poke the peanuts or Styrofoam™ balls to build a structure.

3. Students at each table can work together to create a group structure.

4. Model for the students some ideas on how to get started, by making a base first for the bottom and building up so objects don't fall.

Areas of Fine-Motor Development	
	Visual-Motor Integration
	Pencil Grip
	Cutting Skills
X	Eye-Hand Coordination
X	Hand Strength

---

40 Perler® Bead Creations

Materials Needed:

- ☐ class set of shaped Perler® Pegboards (heart, star, circle, square, etc.)
- ☐ 6,000 Perler® Beads
- ☐ several tweezers
- ☐ option for younger children: Use Biggie Bead Pegboards and Perler® Beads

Directions:

1. Demonstrate how to put the Perler® beads on the shaped pegboard.

2. Give each student one shaped pegboard to work with on a table. Place a container of Perler beads in the center of the table for the students to share.

3. Next have them take one Perler bead at a time and place it on a peg on the shaped pegboard.

4. They can fill in the whole shape; make a pattern going around the shape, or use different colors to make a fun creation on the shaped pegboard.

★ **For more of a challenge,** have students use a pair of tweezers to pick up the Perler® beads one at a time and place them on the shaped pegboard.

Areas of Fine-Motor Development	
X	Visual-Motor Integration
	Pencil Grip
	Cutting Skills
X	Eye-Hand Coordination
X	Hand Strength *(pincher grasp)*

Finger Funatics
Activity Card

Fine Motor Development Program

www.fingerfunatics.com

© Shannon Samulski, 2010

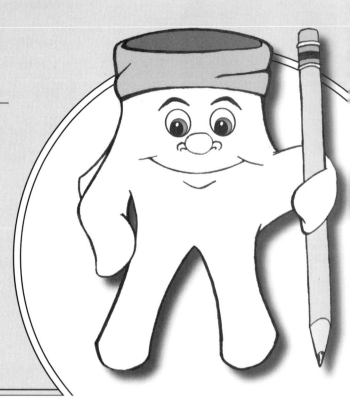

Finger Funatics
Activity Card

Fine Motor Development Program

www.fingerfunatics.com

© Shannon Samulski, 2010

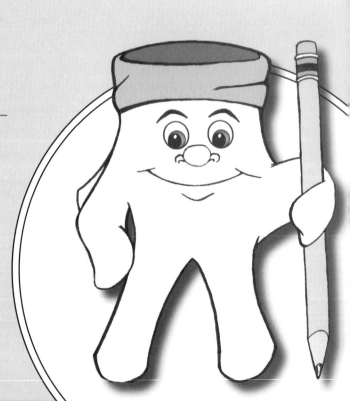

41 Twisty Ties

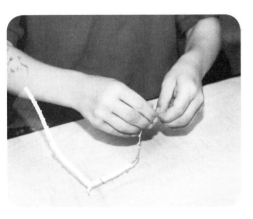

Materials Needed:

☐ bag of twist ties (per student or group)

Directions:

1. Students can make designs out of twist ties by twisting the ends together. This can be a difficult task for some children.

2. They need to pinch and twist using the tips of their fingers.

3. They can create a twist tie chain, create letters, creatures, etc. (Be sure to throw away twist ties that have wires coming out to prevent scratching/poking.)

	Areas of Fine-Motor Development
	Visual-Motor Integration
	Pencil Grip
	Cutting Skills
X	Eye-Hand Coordination
X	Hand Strength

42 Pick-Up Sticks

Materials Needed:

☐ Pick-Up Sticks sets—enough for two children to share a set

Directions:

1. Pair up the students in groups of two or three and give each group a set of Pick-Up Sticks.

2. Demonstrate how to play the game first.

3. Have one student hold all the sticks in a bundle about one inch from the floor or table top.

4. Have the students take turns picking up one stick at a time without moving any of the others. If they are successful they may go again. If they move a stick, they lose their turn.

5. Make sure they always keep a close eye on the sticks!

Note: If they are having difficulty, students can use their sticks to help lift a stick from the pile.

	Areas of Fine-Motor Development
X	Visual-Motor Integration
	Pencil Grip
	Cutting Skills
	Eye-Hand Coordination
X	Hand Strength *(pincher grasp)*

Finger Funatics
Activity Card

Fine Motor Development Program

www.fingerfunatics.com

© Shannon Samulski, 2010

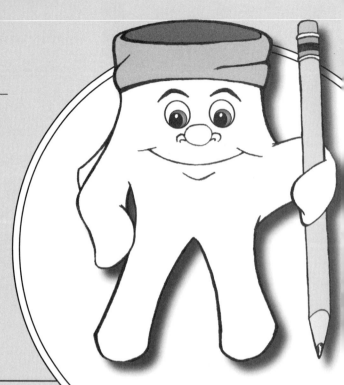

Finger Funatics
Activity Card

Fine Motor Development Program

www.fingerfunatics.com

© Shannon Samulski, 2010

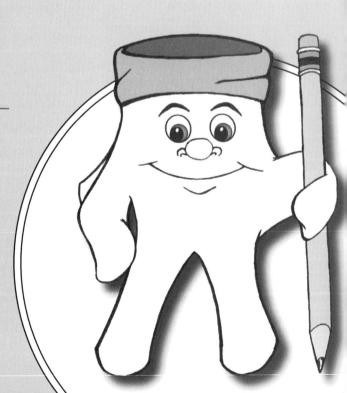

43 PixOs™

Areas of Fine-Motor Development	
	Visual-Motor Integration
	Pencil Grip
	Cutting Skills
X	Eye-Hand Coordination
X	Hand Strength (pincher grasp)

Materials Needed:

☐ individual set of PixOs™ sets (PixOs™ tray, templates, and PixOs™ beads) for each student

☐ spray bottle of water

☐ tweezers or PixOs™ pen (optional)

Directions:

1. Have each student pick out a template and tray to use in her workstation.

2. Place a container of different colored PixOs™ beads at each table.

3. Students will put the corresponding colored PixOs™ onto the templates, continuing until they have completed the template. For more of a challenge they can use tweezers or the PixOs™ pen to place beads.

4. Once the design is complete, have students use water bottles to spray their work. Let it dry and they can take it home.

44 Punch Crazy

Areas of Fine-Motor Development	
	Visual-Motor Integration
	Pencil Grip
	Cutting Skills
X	Eye-Hand Coordination
X	Hand Strength (pincher grasp)

Materials Needed:

☐ bin of giant and small shape punches (star, heart, snowflake, hand, foot, etc.)

☐ hand punches (tears, dragonfly, square, triangle, etc.)

☐ class set of paper punches with grips

☐ several sheets of paper with a letter, number, name, or word in large print

☐ scrap paper (to punch out)

Directions:

1. Pass out to each student a punch, scrap paper, and a sheet of paper with letters and numbers on it in large print.

2. Have the students punch out several shapes from scrap paper.

3. Have them place the shapes along the line of their letter, number, name, or word until the lines are covered with punched out shapes.

4. Encourage them to be patient and keep going.

Finger Funatics
Activity Card

Fine Motor Development Program

www.fingerfunatics.com

© Shannon Samulski, 2010

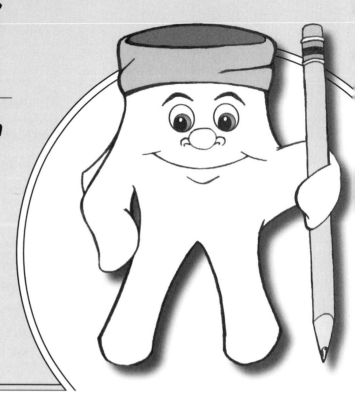

Finger Funatics
Activity Card

Fine Motor Development Program

www.fingerfunatics.com

© Shannon Samulski, 2010

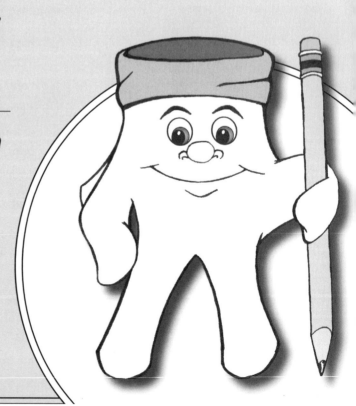

45 Jumbo Jacks

Materials Needed:

- [ ] jumbo jacks set with ball—one set per two students
- [ ] option for younger students: use jumbo jacks without ball

Directions:

1. Demonstrate how to play the game of jacks by bouncing the ball and grabbing one jack; bounce the ball and grab two jacks, etc.

2. For younger students or students having difficulty spread out the jacks and instead of bouncing the ball have them clap one and grab one jack in one scoop; clap two and grab two jacks in one scoop, etc.

3. Children can practice having spinning jack races on a table. Each student will begin to spin a jack, the child whose jack spins longer wins.

	Areas of Fine-Motor Development
	Visual-Motor Integration
	Pencil Grip
	Cutting Skills
X	Eye-Hand Coordination
X	Hand Strength

46 Link It Up

Materials Needed:

- [ ] bin of colored chain links
- [ ] index cards
- [ ] single hole punch
- [ ] marker

Directions:

1. Give each child a pile of colored chain links, several 3x5 cards, a marker, and a single hole punch.

2. Have child write a number on his card (1-20 depending on the age of the student)

3. Next, have the child punch a hole (assist if needed) in the bottom right-hand corner of the card.

4. Next, have the child link together in a chain the matching number of links to the number card, working on one-to-one correspondence.

5. Option: Have students create a link chain pattern with the colored links and describe their patterns to you.

6. Option: Have students estimate the length of various items in the room. For example, is a tissue box 5 chain lengths long? 7 chain lengths long? Test their estimates by creating a link chain the same length as the object.

	Areas of Fine-Motor Development
	Visual-Motor Integration
	Pencil Grip
	Cutting Skills
X	Eye-Hand Coordination
X	Hand Strength

Finger Funatics
Activity Card

Fine Motor Development Program

www.fingerfunatics.com

© Shannon Samulski, 2010

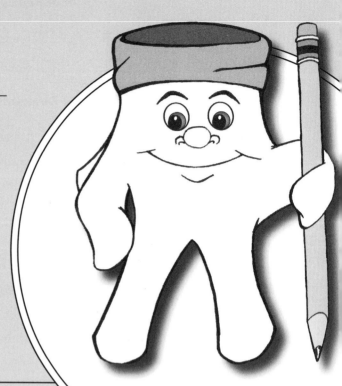

Finger Funatics
Activity Card

Fine Motor Development Program

www.fingerfunatics.com

© Shannon Samulski, 2010

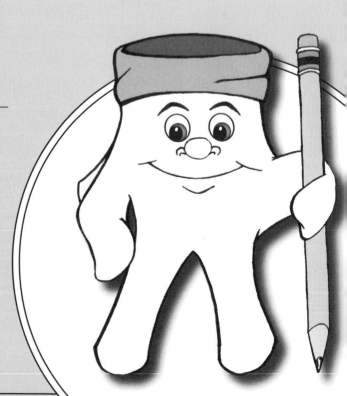

47 Dizzy Tops

■ Materials Needed:

- ☐ spinning tops

■ Directions:

1. Give each student a spinning top and demonstrate how to spin the top.

2. Have them practice spinning the top on a hard surface to see how long they can keep the top spinning. Have them try to catch the handle of the top with their index finger, middle finger, and thumb together while the top is spinning.

3. **Option:** Children can race each other to see who can spin their top the longest.

★ **For more of a challenge,** encourage students to try spinning the top with different fingers (e.g., middle finger/thumb).

Areas of Fine-Motor Development	
	Visual-Motor Integration
	Pencil Grip
	Cutting Skills
X	Eye-Hand Coordination
X	Hand Strength

48 Mini LITE-BRITE™

■ Materials Needed:

- ☐ Mini LITE-BRITE™ or LITE-BRITE™ Cube
- ☐ 50+ LITE-BRITE™ pegs per students
- ☐ optional: LITE-BRITE™ all-paper template

■ Directions:

1. Give each child a Mini LITE-BRITE™ or have students work in table groups with the LITE-BRITE Cube™ style. Each child will need 50+ LITE-BRITE™ All Pegs to work with.

2. Demonstrate how to use the LITE-BRITE™, how to hold the pegs to push into the holes, etc. (Note: the Mini LITE-BRITE™ turns off after three minutes of use.)

3. Let students create letters, numbers, or designs; or use the LITE- BRITE™ All Paper to create a template.

★ **For more of a challenge,** encourage students to push in the pegs with different finger combinations (such as thumb and pointer, thumb and middle finger, etc.)

Areas of Fine-Motor Development	
	Visual-Motor Integration
	Pencil Grip
	Cutting Skills
X	Eye-Hand Coordination
X	Hand Strength

Finger Funatics
Activity Card

Fine Motor Development Program

www.fingerfunatics.com

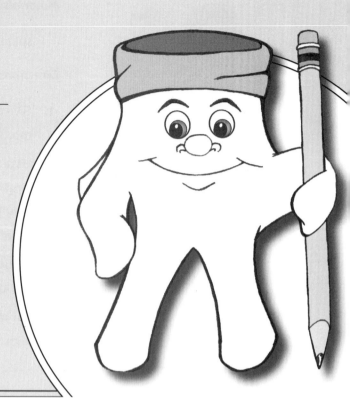

Finger Funatics
Activity Card

Fine Motor Development Program

www.fingerfunatics.com

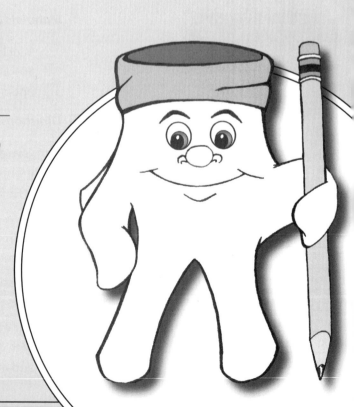

49 Creampuff

Materials Needed:

- ☐ 5"x7" or larger piece of card board or tag board
- ☐ shaving cream (travel size preferred)
- ☐ individual glue bottles (2 oz.)
- ☐ sprinkles
- ☐ marker

Directions:

1. Give each child a piece of cardboard and marker. Have her write a letter, shape, or word on the cardboard. For younger students the template can be made for them.

2. Then have the children outline their objects with shaving cream. Encourage them to stay on the pattern line created with the marker. (Younger students may need assistance in operating the shaving cream can.)

3. Next have them outline the shaving cream line in glue. If you are using mini individual glue bottles, encourage students to hold them in a pencil grip style.

4. Once they have completed both the shaving cream and glue line have students gently swirl the glue and shaving cream together.

5. Finally, have them place the sprinkles on their work. For a challenge, have them use their pincher grasp to put the sprinkles on using different finger combinations.

6. Students will be amazed that their art work will become puffy as it dries.

Areas of Fine-Motor Development	
	Visual-Motor Integration
X	Pencil Grip
	Cutting Skills
X	Eye-Hand Coordination
X	Hand Strength

50 Squirt!

Materials Needed:

- ☐ spray bottles filled with water
- ☐ food coloring
- ☐ white butcher paper

Directions:

1. Start off with enough empty spray bottles for each student or for two students to share. Model the appropriate way to use the spray bottle. Have them practice the motion of pulling the lever the back and forth to squirt.

2. Fill each bottle with water and a few drops of food coloring (give children different colors). On a sidewalk spread out a roll of white butcher paper or individual white sheets. The students can spray the water on the paper to make designs, and build hand strength while operating the sprayers.

3. During the winter they can spray the snow different colors and build hand strength while operating the bottle.

4. In the spring, have students use the spray bottles to take turns watering plants at school or home.

Areas of Fine-Motor Development	
	Visual-Motor Integration
	Pencil Grip
	Cutting Skills
	Eye-Hand Coordination
X	Hand Strength

Finger Funatics
Activity Card

Fine Motor Development Program

www.fingerfunatics.com

© Shannon Samulski, 2010

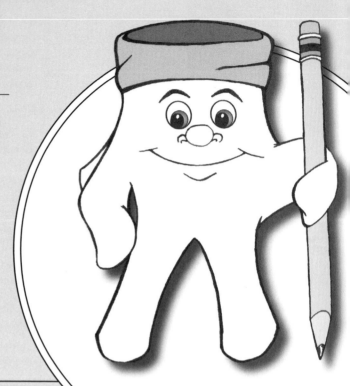

Finger Funatics
Activity Card

Fine Motor Development Program

www.fingerfunatics.com

© Shannon Samulski, 2010

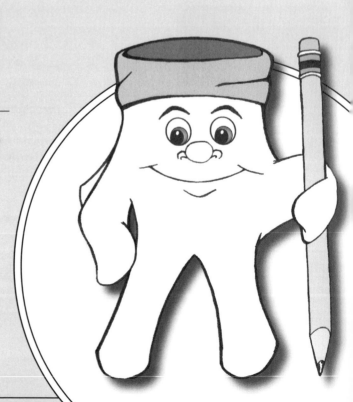

Take-Home Kit

Developed by Shannon Samulski

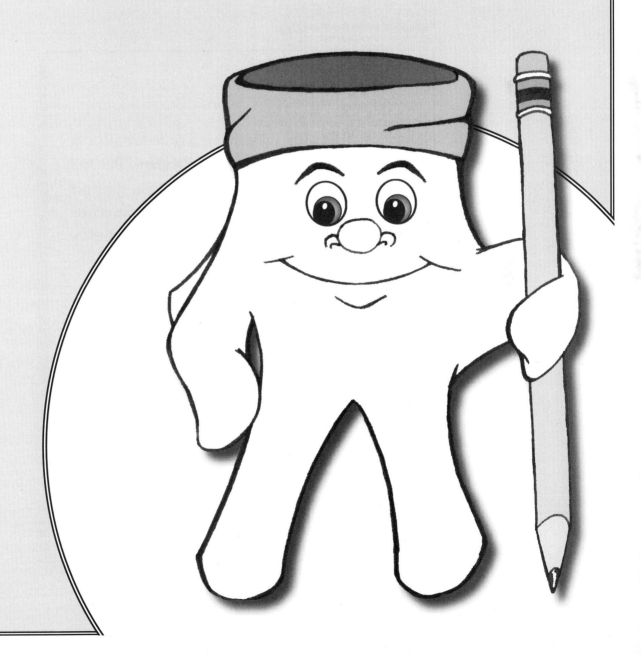

Finger Funatics Take-Home Kit

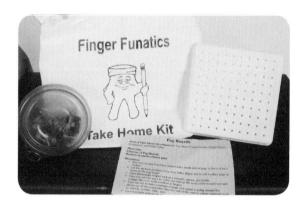

For children needing extra practice outside of school, create a Finger Funatics Take-Home Kit using the activity cards and materials provided in the program.

Teachers can create Finger Funatics kits using large reclosable plastic bags, or plastic storage containers. A laminated activity card and related materials are included in each kit. One or more activities can be sent home at a time, or a checkout rotation for all the kits can be created for students needing more practice.

Sample Letter for Families:

Dear_____,

I am working on developing my fine motor skills at school with the **Finger Funatics Program**. This will help me with my handwriting, cutting skills, eye-hand coordination and my grasp. I am working on fun activities that are fun and we can do together. Each activity has a direction card and the materials needed to complete the task.

I will get a **Finger Funatics Take-Home Kit** each week. At the end of the week we can return it and trade it for a new activity.

Let's set aside at least 5-10 minutes a day and have fun together!

Thank you for your help!

Materials List

The materials for Finger Funatics are designed to be mostly consumable items commonly available within your classroom, school or home. Some of the materials are used in several activities.

Play-Doh® or Funatic-Doh (see recipe on page 77)	4" x 6" index cards
small beads (pea size or smaller)	pom-pons or cotton balls
larger beads (larger than a pea)	pipe cleaners
children's scissors	construction paper (variety of colors)
variety of buttons	old holiday cards
shoelaces, yarn, or string	paper cups
single hole punch	twist ties
small margarine tub and lid	Cheerios®/Kix®/Fruit Loops® cereal
variety of dry beans (kidney, pinto, etc.)	glue
pint size or larger water bottles	glue sticks
tweezers (optional)	sponges
clothes pins	buckets
playing cards	thumb tacks
large and small paperclips	foam paper
markers	paper plates
crayons	dry erase erasers
noodles (penne)	shaving cream
pennies	glitter or glitter glue sticks
card stock	large craft sticks
waxed paper	sprinkles
stencils (any type)	variety of beads or craft jewels
paper	

Purchasable Materials Suggestion List $10 and under

Below is a list of approximate prices and suggested websites where you can find materials that are referenced in the Finger Funatics Program.

Item	Approximate Price	Suggested Website
Mini LITE-BRITE™	$9.99	http://www.hasbrotoyshop.com
Barrel of Monkeys™	$6.99	http://www.toysrus.com
Pick up sticks	$6.50	http://www.amazon.com
Jumbo jacks	$5.99	http://www.orientaltrading.com
Pix-Os™	$6.99	http://www.toysrus.com
Colored chain links	$3.45	http://www.enasco.com
Perler® Bead	$3.99	http://www.koolstuff4kids.com
Biggie Bead pegboards Perler Beads®	$5.99	http://www.koolstuff4kids.com
Geo-board	$3.30	http://sciencekit.com
Peg board	$6.99	http://www.amazon.com
Spinning tops	$3.99 a dozen	http://www.orientaltrading.com
Alphabet stamps	$5.99	http://www.orientialtrading.com
Scrapbook punch	$8.99	http://cropping corner.com

Funatic-Doh Recipe

2 ½ cups flour

½ cup salt

1 Tbsp. alum or cream of tartar

2 packages of unsweetened any flavor of Kool-Aid®

Mix all the ingredients then add:

3 Tbsp. oil

2 cups of boiling water

Stir until mixed well. Knead on a floured surface.

You may need to add more flour to get the right consistency.

Store in a sealed, reclosable plastic bag to keep fresh for repeated use.

Blackline Masters

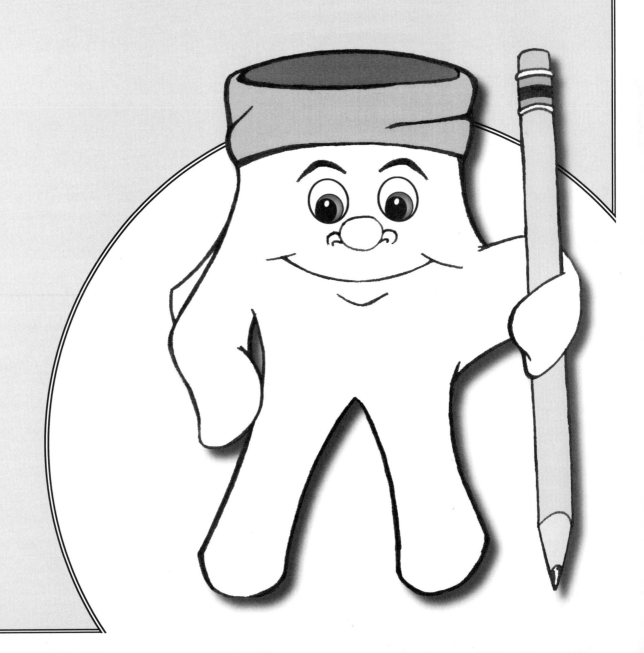

Cutting Skills Assessment

Directions: Have the student cut out the circle on the black line.

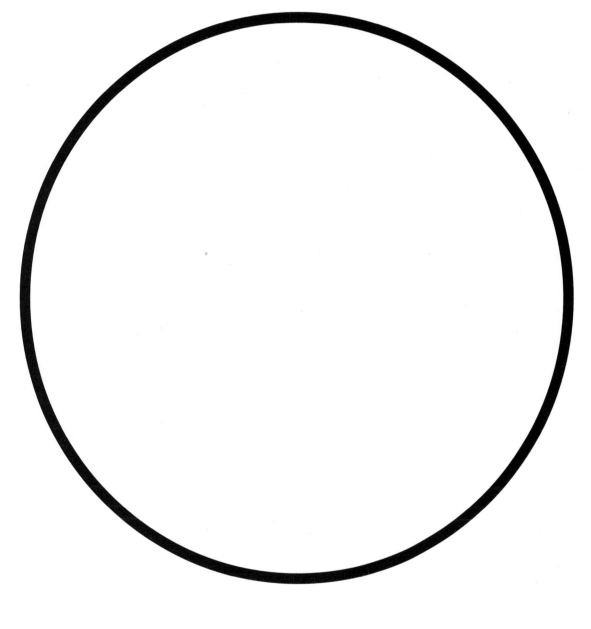

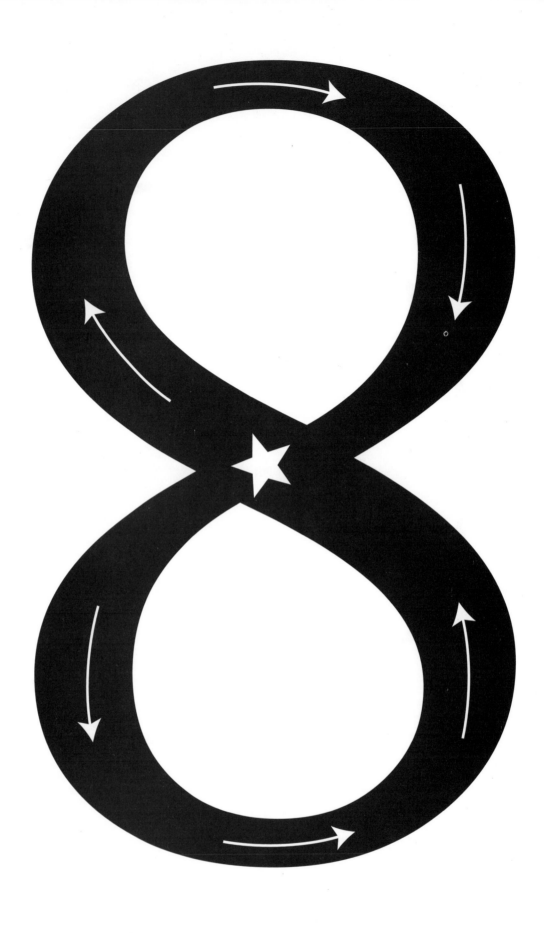

Crazy Lazy 8

L C O X R G N
J Q U B Y P T
N W D V M H S
A F Z I E K S

3 11 15 7 19 16
6 18 14 2 10
16 8 20 12 4
10 1 5 17 13 9 4

Top grid (numbers):

4	9	13	17	5	1	10
12						2
20						14
8						18
16	19	7	15	11	3	6

Bottom grid (letters):

S	K	E	I	Z	F	A	T
H							P
M							Y
V							B
D							U
W							Q
N	G	R	X	O	C	L	J

Appendix

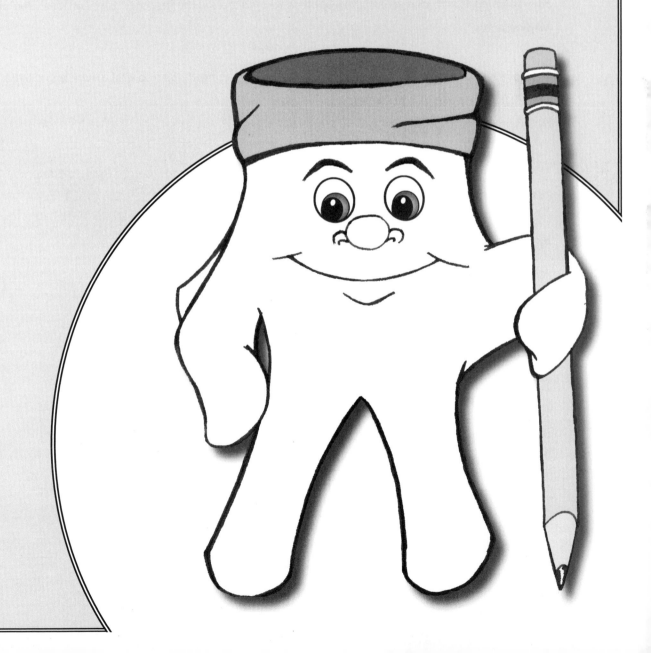

References/Recommended Reading

Activities for Fine Motor Skill Development by Jodene Smith, 2004

Ready-to-Use Fine Motor and Handwriting Activities for Young Children by Joanne Landy & Keith Burridge, 2000

Why Motor Skills Matter: Improve Your Child's Physical Development to Enhance Learning and Self-Esteem by Tara Losquardo Liddle & Laura Yorke

Learning in Motion: 101+ Sensory Activities for the Classroom by Patricia Angermeier, Joan Krzyzanowski, and Kristina Keller Moir, 2009

Early Learning Standards and Staff Development: Best Practices in the Face of Change by Gaye Gronlund and Marlyn James, 2007

The 2,000 Best Games and Activities, 2E: Using Play to Teach Curiosity, Self-Control, Kindness and Other Essential Life Skills (2,000 Best Games & Activities)
by Susan Kettmann, 2005

The Out-of-Sync Child: Recognizing and Coping with Sensory Processing Disorder, Revised Edition by Carol Kranowitz and Lucy Jane Miller, 2006

Ready to Write, Nancy Sornson Early Learning Foundation, 2010

Special Acknowledgments

Photographs Compliments of:

John Kemski, Owner
Express Photo & Camera
37108 6 Mile Road
Livonia, MI 48152-2777
Phone: (734) 591-9533
www.expressphotodigital.com

Artwork Compliments of:

Joshua Carpenter, Freelance Artist and Cartoonist
Email: comicjlee25@yahoo.com

Editor:

Linda Wacyk

Graphic Designer:

Kate de Fuccio

Photo Shoot Participants:

Wondergarten Friends in Mrs. Black's classroom
Our Pre-School Pals
Mrs. Lupton's K-1 Summer School Class

Thank you to:

—*Lena Montgomery for making this happen.*
—*Bob and Nancy Sornson for the many revisions and continued guidance.*

About the Author

Shannon Samulski is an educational consultant, special education teacher, Early Learning Success Facilitator, and national presenter. She is well known for her practical information and enthusiastic style, and her experience with Response to Intervention, data-driven instruction, numeracy, differentiation, and instructional consultation. Shannon can be contacted to schedule a staff training at samulski@comcast.net.